12/

Gloria —

Happy Holidays!

Enjoy!

Ariel

IF I CAN COOK /
YOU KNOW GOD CAN

WORKS BY

NTOZAKE SHANGE

{PLAYS}

For Colored Girls Who Have Considered Suicide When the Rainbow Is Enuf

Three Pieces

{NOVELS}

Sassafrass, Cypress & Indigo

Betsey Brown

Liliane: Resurrection of the Daughter

{POETRY}

The Love Space Demands: A Continuing Saga

Nappy Edges

A Daughter's Geography

Ridin' the Moon in Texas

{NONFICTION}

If I Can Cook / You Know God Can

{CHILDREN'S}

I Live in Music (poetry)

Whitewash (nonfiction)